CHAFING DISH POSSIBILITIES

Chafing Dish Possibilities

BY

FANNIE MERRITT FARMER

Principal of the Boston Cooking School

AND AUTHOR OF

" THE BOSTON COOKING SCHOOL COOK BOOK "

They eat, they drink, and in communion sweet
Quaff immortality and joy
MILTON

Creative Cookbooks
Monterey, California

Chafing Dish Possibilities

by
Fannie Merritt Farmer

ISBN: 1-58963-547-7

Copyright © 2001 by Fredonia Books

Reprinted from the 1918 edition

Creative Cookbooks
An Imprint of Fredonia Books
Monterey, California
http://www.creativecookbooks.com

To the Memory of

CARRIE M. DEARBORN

MY DEVOTED FRIEND AND EARNEST CO-WORKER,
THIS BOOK IS LOVINGLY DEDICATED
BY THE AUTHOR

Blest be the spot, where cheerful guests retire,
To pause from toil, and trim their evening fire;
Blest that abode, where want and pain repair,
And every stranger finds a ready chair;
Blest be those feasts with simple plenty crown'd,
Where all the ruddy family around
Laugh at the jests of pranks that never fail,
Or sigh with pity at some mournful tale,
Or press the bashful stranger to his food,
And learn the luxury of doing good!

GOLDSMITH

We may live without poetry, music, and art;
We may live without conscience, and live without heart;
We may live without friends, we may live without books;
But civilized man cannot live without cooks.
He may live without books, — what is knowledge but
      grieving?
He may live without hope, — what is hope but deceiving?
He may live without love, — what is passion but pining?
But where is the man that can live without dining?

OWEN MEREDITH

TABLE OF CONTENTS

GLIMPSES OF CHAFING DISHES
IN THE PAST

And often a retrospect delights the mind

DANTE

Chafing Dish Possibilities

&

I

THERE seems to exist in the minds of many the wholly to be contradicted notion that the chafing dish is a utensil of modern invention. Although its origin is enveloped in darkness, "looking backward o'er the ages" many allusions are made to its use.

Imagine, if you can, the Israelites, those dwellers in tents, feasting upon the locusts of Egypt and Palestine cooked in a utensil corresponding in many particulars to the chafing dish of the present day.

Among the ruins of Pompeii have been found bronze chafing dishes of unique designs and careful workmanship, which give undisputed proof of their use in this city, which contained the villas of many wealthy Romans. What a rich store of knowledge concerning Roman home life has been gained from these excavations!

13

Chafing Dish Possibilities

Mommsen, in his "Römische Geschichte," refers to the lavish display at the tables of the Romans, and affirms that expense was never considered in their hospitality. In those days, he asserts, "A well-wrought bronze cooking machine came to cost more than an estate." What a trifling difference between these and our modern chafing dishes!

The history of France, that land to which we ever look for gastronomic delights, furnishes many an illustration of the high esteem in which chafing dishes have been held by many of the mightiest of their land.

Louis XV., according to Goncourt, took much delight in cooking, and often amused himself "by making quintessential stews in silver pans." The palate of Louis XVI. was often tickled by "piping hot dishes, brought in on a chafing dish."

Napoleon Bonaparte, when laying down the affairs of war and enjoying for a short period the joys of home life, has cooked, — as Baron Meneval writes, — in a silver chafing dish, an omelet for the enjoyment of the empress and himself.

Madame Récamier, the beautiful and intellectual society leader, whose salon was always filled with a brilliant circle, entertained by the

Chafing Dishes in the Past

use of a chafing dish; and many an historic speech has been made during the preparation of some viand fit for the gods.

Madame de Staël, "the greatest woman in literary history," when exiled by Napoleon Bonaparte from her beloved France, took with her, among household treasures, the chafing dish which played a not unimportant part in her Paris entertainments.

Glancing at the lives of some of England's greatest literary men, it is found that a faithful history of the London clubs to which they belonged, reveals the history of their manners and their ways. From the time that Sir Walter Raleigh founded the "Mermaid" to the days of the famous "Literary Club," chafing dishes have appeared more or less conspicuously on the tables of those giants of old, where —

> "Mingled with the friendly bowl,
> The feast of reason and the flow of soul."

"I regard the discovery of a new dish as a far more interesting event than the discovery of a star; for we have always stars enough, but we can never have too many dishes." If there are still those of this same opinion, with a chafing dish for a companion, cannot they work their way to fame?

CHAFING DISH SUGGESTIONS

He who receives friends without himself bestowing some pains upon the repast prepared for them, does not deserve to have friends

                                        BRILLAT-SAVARIN

II

CHAFING DISH SUGGESTIONS

THE chafing dish of to-day has accomplished
much as a civilizer, seeming to rekindle the
flames of hospitality and to elevate the stand-
ard of cookery. Who can doubt its permanent
stay!.

The bachelor feels himself proud to be called
the pioneer in the use of this utensil. All must
agree that epicureanism belongs to the lords of
creation, and many an one has made himself
quite famous by compounding some dish for
"those palates who must have inventions to
delight the taste."

The broader and more valuable use of the
chafing dish has asserted itself, and now it is
found in the well-conducted home, where its
appearance at the breakfast table means the
cooking of eggs to perfection; at the lunch
table, the savory rechauffé. The chafing dish
should not find a place on the table when a
ceremonial dinner is served; but in the household where but one maid is kept, the Thursday
night meal is often anticipated on account of

Chafing Dish Possibilities

its use. When the eye of the convalescent brightens and his appetite is stimulated by a choice tidbit prepared on the chafing dish, then its value is most appreciated, and it is considered among the indispensables. All in all, the chafing dish is most happily in evidence when congenial spirits meet to make glad after "the lamps are lit," and "small cheer and great welcome make a merry feast."

So many and varied are the styles of chafing dishes, one must be governed by his taste and the extent of his purse strings in making a selection. Comparatively few can enjoy the luxury of a silver or silver-plated dish, so the choice lies between agate ware, nickel-plated, copper, or brass ones. The last two kinds mentioned are not recommended, as much time needs be expended to keep them brightly polished. If a moderate-priced dish is desired, preference is shown for the nickel-plated. Nickel-plated dishes are very attractive and may be easily kept clean and bright by washing in hot, soapy water, wiping dry with a soft towel, and rubbing with a piece of chamois skin or cotton flannel.

The lower pan of the late chafing dish (known as the hot-water pan or bath) is supplied with two handles, which prove of great advantage

Chafing Dish Suggestions

in moving the pan when heated. An accident from burning, in the household of a manufacturer, suggested this valuable addition of handles, and also the addition of a tray on which to place this pan.

The upper pan, familiarly called the blazer, is furnished with a long wooden handle, and is more often used alone than with the hot-water pan. The hot-water pan, however, plays a necessary part, when the dish to be prepared contains eggs, or eggs and milk in combination, which should always be cooked at a low temperature. It is also of use to keep the viand hot, without further cooking, that a second serve may be as satisfactory as the first. The flame of the lamp should always be extinguished, as soon as the cooking is accomplished.

A circular chafing dish is supplied with one lamp, the wick of which is asbestos, covered with a fine wire netting. The flame is regulated by metal slides, which are controlled by an adjustable screw. The average lamp holds about one gill of alcohol, and will burn about one and one-half hours. Oval chafing dishes, which are not commonly used, are supplied with two or three lamps, the wicks of which are cotton lamp-wicking. The flame is regulated by turning the wicks by means of an adjustable screw.

Chafing Dish Possibilities

The best grade of alcohol, known as high proof spirits, is recommended for chafing dish use. It gives more heat, burns without an odor, and proves less expensive than an inferior quality. It is taken for granted that alcohol is to furnish the fuel, for the days of live coals and oil have passed away, and the days of gas and electricity are not yet at hand for those of moderate means.

With a chafing dish outfit, an ambition naturally arises to collect pretty bowls and odd pitchers of various sizes, dainty jars and covered dishes to hold seasonings and condiments, and other unique choice pieces of china that may prove useful.

The glass or granite ware measuring cups, divided into thirds and quarters, are absolutely necessary, as are tea and table spoons for measuring. Let it be remembered that level measurements are called for in the recipes contained in the following chapters of this little book. It must never be forgotten that accurate measurements are essential for good results. "Trifles make perfection, but perfection is no trifle."

As chafing dish cookery should be done as noiselessly as possible, a long-handled wooden spoon proves a desirable utensil during the prep-

Chafing Dish Suggestions

aration of the dish; while the large spoon with ebony handle may be reserved for the serving.

The chafing dish should be placed on a metal tray, previous to the filling of the lamp, thus avoiding all danger of accident after lighting, should a draft of air or the expansion of the heated fuel cause the flame to spread outward and downward. This tray also serves as a protection for the table, and admits of an easy removal of the dish when desired.

He who most carefully anticipates the pleasure of his family or guests has much preparatory work done. As far as possible the ingredients should be measured and mixed before the assembly of the party, and it is well if they be placed on the table or tray by the hands of the one who is to do the cooking, that " he may laugh as the play goes on."

Accept as a final suggestion the plan of measuring butter by tablespoons and making into balls by the use of butter hands. These balls will keep in good shape if allowed to remain in a cold place until needed.

TOAST, GRIDDLE CAKES, AND
FRITTERS

He that will have a cake out of wheat, must needs tarry at the grinding

SHAKESPEARE

26

III

TOAST, GRIDDLE CAKES, AND FRITTERS

Milk Toast

MELT two tablespoons butter, add two and one-half tablespoons flour, and, when well mixed, pour on gradually two cups milk. Season with one-half teaspoon salt, and stir constantly until mixture thickens. Have at hand six slices of toasted bread. Dip slices separately in sauce, when soft remove to serving plate, and pour over each slice one tablespoon sauce.

Tomato Cream Toast

Melt two tablespoons butter, add two tablespoons flour, mixed with one-half teaspoon salt, and pour on gradually one and one-half cups stewed and strained tomatoes, to which has been added one-fourth teaspoon soda; then add one-half cup cream. Dip slices of toasted bread in sauce, and serve same as Milk Toast. This sauce should be cooked over hot water.

27

Chafing Dish Possibilities

Egg Toast

Melt one tablespoon butter, add one table-spoon flour mixed with one-half teaspoon salt and one-eighth teaspoon pepper, and pour on gradually one cup milk. Add the whites of three hard-boiled eggs, finely chopped. Pour over four slices of toasted bread, and sprinkle the top with the yolks of three hard-boiled eggs forced through a potato ricer or strainer.

Anchovy Toast

Toast four slices of bread from which the crusts have been removed and spread with an-chovy paste. Scald one cup milk, add two egg yolks, and stir constantly until the mixture thickens. Beat the whites of two eggs until stiff, add to the thickened milk, beat thoroughly and pour over the toast.

German Toast

Beat two eggs slightly, add one-third teaspoon salt, one and one-half tablespoons sugar and two-thirds cup milk; strain. Soak four slices stale bread in mixture until soft. Heat and brown delicately on both sides in a hot blazer, using enough butter to prevent burning.

28

Toast, Griddle Cakes, and Fritters

Brewis

Break stale pieces of brown bread in small pieces. Butter a hot chafing dish, put in bread, and add milk to cover. Cook until mixture is smooth, which may be accomplished by mashing pieces with a fork during the cooking; season with butter and salt.

Entire Wheat Griddle Cakes

Mix and sift one-half cup flour, one-fourth cup coarse entire wheat or Graham flour, one and one-half teaspoons baking powder, one and one-half tablespoons sugar, and one-fourth teaspoon salt. Add one-half cup milk, one egg slightly beaten, and one-half tablespoon melted butter. Drop from the tip of a spoon on a hot, well-buttered blazer. Cook on one side until delicately browned; turn and cook on the other side.

French Fritters

Mix and sift one cup flour, one-fourth teaspoon salt, and two teaspoons baking powder. Add three-fourths cup milk, one egg well beaten, and one tablespoon melted butter. Fry same as griddle cakes. When cooked, spread with currant jelly, roll, and sprinkle with powdered sugar. Beat jelly with a fork, before attempting to spread.

29

EGGS

And eggs — even they have their moral. See how they come and go. Every pleasure is transitory. We can't even eat long

DICKENS

IV

EGGS

Boiled Eggs

WHEN water boils in blazer carefully put in with a spoon the number of eggs desired, having sufficient water to cover them. Cover and place over hot-water pan, that eggs may cook in water at the proper temperature. Cook from seven to eight minutes if preferred "soft boiled."

Poached Eggs

Have blazer two-thirds full of boiling water. Break each egg separately into a saucer, and slip into the pan. Cover and place blazer over hot water pan. Let stand until whites of eggs are firm. Remove from pan to circular pieces of buttered toast. Sprinkle with salt and pepper, and place on top of each one-fourth teaspoon butter.

Eggs à la Finoise

Prepare Poached Eggs and serve with tomato sauce.

33

Chafing Dish Possibilities

Buttered Eggs

Melt three-fourths tablespoon butter in a hot blazer, slip in carefully one egg, sprinkle with salt and pepper, and cook until the white is firm, turning once during the cooking. Attempt to cook but one egg at a time.

Eggs à la Suisse

Melt one tablespoon butter in blazer, add one-half cup thin cream, and as soon as cream reaches the boiling point, slip in carefully three eggs, one at a time. Place over hot water pan, sprinkle with salt and pepper and a few grains cayenne. When whites are nearly firm, sprinkle with grated cheese and finish the cooking. Serve on circular pieces of buttered toast. Strain cream remaining in pan over eggs.

Eggs in Brown Butter

Melt one-half tablespoon each lard and butter in hot blazer. Break one egg in a saucer, and slip carefully into dish. Cook until white is firm, turning egg once. So continue until a sufficient number are cooked. Brown four tablespoons butter, add one tablespoon Tarragon vinegar, one teaspoon Chili sauce, one teaspoon lemon juice, and one-fourth teaspoon salt. Strain over eggs.

34

Eggs

Eggs au Beurre Noir

Melt one tablespoon butter, and slip in carefully four eggs, one at a time. Sprinkle with salt and pepper, and cook until whites are firm, adding more butter if needed. Turn once during the cooking. Brown two tablespoons butter, add one-half teaspoon vinegar, and strain over eggs.

Souffléd Egg

Beat the white of one egg until stiff, and season with salt. Put into a tumbler, and place tumbler in pan of warm water, allowing water to heat gradually until boiling point is reached, when egg is cooked. As the white of egg rises, make a depression and drop in the yolk.

Scrambled Eggs

Beat five eggs slightly, add one-half teaspoon salt, one eighth teaspoon pepper, and one-half cup milk or cream. Melt two tablespoons butter, pour in egg mixture, and cook until of a creamy consistency, stirring constantly and scraping from bottom of pan. Many prefer to omit the milk, and use three tablespoons butter in place of two tablespoons.

35

Chafing Dish Possibilities

Scrambled Eggs with Tomatoes

Fry one small slice onion in two tablespoons butter, five minutes. Add one cup tomatoes, one teaspoon sugar, one-half teaspoon salt, a few grains pepper, and cook five minutes. Add four eggs, slightly beaten, and cook same as Scrambled Eggs. Serve with entire wheat or brown bread toast.

Scrambled Eggs with Anchovy Toast

Spread thin slices of buttered toast with anchovy paste, and cover with scrambled eggs.

Scrambled Eggs with Asparagus Tips

Prepare Scrambled Eggs, and add one cup cooked asparagus tips. If the canned vegetable is used, rinse thoroughly and drain.

Scrambled Eggs with Cheese

Prepare Scrambled Eggs, and just before serving add four tablespoons grated cheese, mixed with one-fourth teaspoon paprika.

Scrambled Eggs with Mushrooms

Clean mushrooms; remove stems, scrape, and break in pieces; peel caps and break in pieces.

Eggs

Melt four tablespoons butter, add one and one-half cups mushrooms, previously dredged with flour, a few drops onion juice, one-fourth teaspoon salt, and a few grains cayenne. Cook eight minutes. Beat four eggs slightly, add one-half teaspoon salt and one-eighth teaspoon pepper; then add to mushrooms and cook until eggs are of a creamy consistency, stirring constantly and scraping from bottom of pan.

Eggs à la Creole

Cook three tablespoons butter with one tablespoon finely chopped onion, three minutes. Add one and three-fourths cups tomatoes, drained from their liquor, and cook eight minutes. Add one tablespoon sliced mushrooms, one tablespoon capers, one-fourth teaspoon salt, a few grains of cayenne, and five eggs beaten slightly. Cook until of a creamy consistency, stirring constantly and scraping from bottom of pan.

Eggs à la Caracas

Chop finely two ounces smoked, dried beef, freed from fat and outside skin. Add one cup tomatoes, one-fourth cup grated old English cheese, a few drops onion juice, and a few grains each of cinnamon and cayenne. Melt

37

two tablespoons butter, add mixture, and when heated add three eggs slightly beaten. Cook until of a creamy consistency, stirring constantly and scraping from bottom of pan.

Venetian Eggs

Cook two tablespoons butter with one tablespoon finely chopped onion, a bit of bay leaf, and a blade of mace, until yellow. Remove bay leaf and mace; then add one and one-half cups tomatoes, one-fourth cup cheese cut in small pieces, three eggs slightly beaten, one teaspoon salt, and one-fourth teaspoon paprika. Cook until eggs are of a creamy consistency, stirring constantly and scraping from bottom of pan. Pour over slices of toasted bread.

Eggs à l'Espagnole

Cook a clove of garlic finely chopped, and one-half green pepper finely chopped, in two tablespoons olive oil, five minutes. Add three tomatoes cut in small pieces, eight sliced mushrooms, and one-half cup cold cooked meat, finely chopped. Cook five minutes, add four eggs slightly beaten, and cook until the eggs are set.

Eggs

Curried Eggs

Melt two tablespoons butter, add two tablespoons flour mixed with one-fourth teaspoon salt, one-half teaspoon curry powder, and one-eighth teaspoon paprika. Stir until well mixed, then pour on gradually one cup milk. Add three hard-boiled eggs, cut in eighths lengthwise, and reheat in sauce.

Eggs à la Béchamel

Fry three tablespoons butter with one slice each carrot and onion cut in pieces, a sprig of parsley and a bit of bay leaf, five minutes. Add three tablespoons flour, one-fourth teaspoon salt, and one-eighth teaspoon paprika; then add one cup chicken stock, strain, reheat, and add four hard-boiled eggs, cut in eighths lengthwise. Just before serving, add one-half cup cream and a slight grating of nutmeg.

Eggs à la Soubise

Boil onions and rub through a sieve; there should be one cup of onion purée. Melt two tablespoons butter, add one and one-half tablespoons flour and the onion purée. As soon as heated, add one-third cup milk and the yolks of two eggs. Season with salt and paprika.

Chafing Dish Possibilities

Add five hard-boiled eggs, cut in slices. Just before serving, sprinkle with finely chopped parsley.

Scotch Woodcock

Melt three tablespoons butter, add one and one-half tablespoons flour, and pour on gradually one cup milk. Add one-fourth teaspoon salt, a few grains of cayenne and anchovy essence. Add four hard-boiled eggs, finely chopped, and serve on slices of toast.

Fricasseed Eggs

Cook two tablespoons butter with one and one-half tablespoons finely chopped mushrooms, and one-half shallot, finely chopped. Add one and one-half tablespoons flour, and pour on gradually one cup white stock. Add five hard-boiled eggs cut in slices.

Steamed Eggs

Butter small dario moulds and sprinkle with finely chopped parsley. Carefully slip an egg into each mould, and sprinkle with salt and pepper. Put moulds in blazer, and pour around boiling water to three-fourths the depth of the moulds. Let cook until whites are firm, keeping water below the boiling point. Remove from moulds and serve with tomato sauce.

Eggs

Egg Timbales

Beat four eggs slightly ; add one-fourth cup cream, a few drops of onion juice, one-fourth teaspoon salt, and a few grains each of celery salt and paprika. Turn the mixture into small buttered dario moulds. Set in a pan of hot water and cook until firm. Turn from moulds and serve with a thin tomato or Béchamel sauce.

Plain Omelet

Beat three eggs slightly; add three tablespoons milk, one-third teaspoon salt, and a few grains pepper. Melt one tablespoon butter, turn in the mixture, and cook until of a creamy consistency, using a spatula to scrape cooked mixture from bottom of pan, that it may mix with the uncooked part, and thus prevent any portion from being overdone. Loosen omelet by running spatula around side and bottom of pan. Fold and turn.

Cheese Omelet

Beat two eggs slightly; add one-eighth teaspoon salt and a few grains of cayenne. Melt three-fourths tablespoon butter, pour in mixture, and cook until firm, without stirring. Loosen from pan, roll, and sprinkle with one tablespoon grated cheese.

Chafing Dish Possibilities

Oyster Omelet

Prepare a Plain Omelet. Clean one cup oysters, and cook until plump; drain and reserve liquor. Spread oysters on omelet just before folding. Melt two tablespoons butter; add two tablespoons flour, one-fourth teaspoon salt, and a few grains of pepper. Pour on gradually oyster liquor and enough milk to make one cup liquid. Pour sauce around omelet.

Spanish Omelet

Prepare a Plain Omelet and serve with Spanish Sauce.

Spanish Sauce

Cook two tablespoons butter with one tablespoon finely chopped onion, and one-fourth green pepper (from which the seeds have been removed) finely chopped, five minutes. Add one and three-fourths cups tomatoes, drained from their liquor; cook until moisture has nearly evaporated, then add one tablespoon sliced mushrooms, one tablespoon capers, one-fourth teaspoon salt, and a few grains of cayenne.

OYSTERS

Whom sea-green Sirens from the rocks lament

DRYDEN

V

OYSTERS

Grilled Oysters

CLEAN one pint oysters and drain off all the liquor possible. Put oysters in blazer, and as fast as liquor flows from them, remove it with a spoon. So continue until oysters are plump. Sprinkle with salt and pepper, add two tablespoons butter, and serve on zephyrettes.

Panned Oysters

Melt two and one-half tablespoons butter, add two tablespoons flour, one-fourth teaspoon salt, one-eighth teaspoon paprika, and one-half tablespoon Chili sauce. Clean one pint oysters and add. Cook until edges curl, then add one tablespoon finely chopped parsley and two tablespoons chopped celery. Serve with toast.

Fancy Roast

Clean and drain one pint oysters. Put into a blazer and cook until plump, stirring occasion-

45

ally with a fork. Sprinkle with salt and pepper and add two tablespoons butter. Pour over small slices of toast.

Oyster Fricassee

Clean one pint oysters, reserve liquor, heat to boiling point, and strain through double thickness of cheese-cloth. Add oysters to liquor, and cook until plump, then remove with a skimmer. Add enough cream to liquor to make one cup. Melt two tablespoons butter, add two tablespoons flour, and pour on gradually the liquid. Add one-fourth teaspoon salt, a few grains cayenne, one teaspoon finely chopped parsley, the oysters, and one egg slightly beaten. Serve on toast.

Creamed Oysters

Clean one pint oysters, and cook until plump. Drain, strain the liquor, and add enough milk to make one and one-half cups. Melt three tablespoons butter, add five tablespoons flour, and pour on gradually the liquid. Season with one-half teaspoon salt, and one-eighth teaspoon each pepper and celery salt. Add the oysters, and as soon as heated pour over slices of toast.

Oysters

Celeried Oysters

Prepare same as Creamed Oysters, and after pouring oysters over toast, sprinkle with finely chopped celery.

Oysters in Brown Sauce

Clean one pint oysters and cook until plump; drain, and strain the liquor. Melt one-fourth cup butter, and stir until well browned, add one-fourth cup flour, and stir until flour is browned. Pour on gradually one cup oyster liquor and one-half cup milk. Season with one-half teaspoon salt, one-eighth teaspoon pepper, and one teaspoon anchovy essence. Serve on toast or zephyrettes.

Sauté of Oysters

Clean one pint oysters and cook until plump; drain thoroughly and sprinkle with salt and pepper. Lift each oyster separately, and dip in cracker crumbs. Put three tablespoons butter in blazer, add oysters, brown on one side, turn and brown other side. Serve with horse-radish mustard, which may be bought put up in small jars, of first-class grocers.

Oyster Stew

Clean and drain one pint oysters, reserving liquor. Heat liquor to boiling point, add oysters and cook until plump, care being taken that they are not overdone. Remove oysters with a skimmer, strain liquor a second time, and add to oysters. Scald one pint milk, add oysters with liquor, two tablespoons butter, one teaspoon salt, and a few grains pepper. Serve with oyster crackers, or small pieces of bread, thoroughly toasted. To many the flavor is much improved by cooking with milk a small slice of onion and a stalk of celery broken in pieces; both to be removed as soon as milk is scalded.

Oysters à la Thorndike

Clean and drain one pint oysters. Melt three tablespoons butter, add oysters, and cook until plump; then add one-half teaspoon salt, one-eighth tea-spoon paprika, a slight grating nutmeg, one-fourth cup cream, and yolks of two eggs. Cook until slightly thickened, and serve on zephyrettes.

Devilled Oysters, I.

Clean one pint oysters, drain, and cook until plump. Remove tough muscles from oysters and reserve oyster liquor. Melt three tablespoons butter, add three tablespoons flour, and pour on gradually the oyster liquor with enough water to make one cup liquid. Season with one-

Oysters

half teaspoon salt, one-fourth teaspoon mustard, a few grains cayenne, and one teaspoon lemon juice. As soon as oysters are heated, add the yolk of one egg and one teaspoon finely chopped parsley.

Devilled Oysters, II.

Clean one pint oysters, cook until plump, drain, and reserve liquor. Strain liquor through cheese-cloth. Melt three tablespoons butter, add four tablespoons flour mixed with one-half teaspoon each salt and curry powder, and one-eighth teaspoon paprika. Pour on gradually the oyster liquor with enough water to make one and one-half cups liquid. Add oysters and season with one teaspoon Worcestershire sauce, one tablespoon lemon juice, ten drops Tabasco sauce, and salt to taste. Serve on Graham toast.

Oysters à la D'Uxelles

Clean one pint oysters, heat to boiling point, drain, and reserve liquor. Strain liquor through cheese-cloth; there should be three-fourths cup. Cook two tablespoons butter with two tablespoons chopped canned mushrooms, five minutes. Add two tablespoons flour and pour on gradually the oyster liquor. Season with one-half teaspoon salt, a few grains cayenne, and one teaspoon lemon juice. Add oysters, and, as soon as heated, the yolk of one egg and one table-spoon sherry wine.

Oysters à la Béchamel

Clean one pint oysters and cook until plump. Drain, reserve liquor, and strain through cheese-cloth. Melt three tablespoons butter, add three tablespoons flour, and pour on gradually one-half cup each oyster liquor and highly seasoned chicken stock. Add one-half teaspoon salt, one-eighth teaspoon paprika, the oysters, and one-half cup cream. Serve on zephyrettes.

Curried Oysters

Clean one pint oysters and cook until plump. Drain, reserve liquor, and strain through cheese-cloth. Cook three tablespoons butter with one-half tablespoon onion until yellow. Add four tablespoons flour mixed with one and one-half teaspoons curry powder, one-half teaspoon salt, and one-eighth teaspoon paprika. Pour on gradually oyster liquor and enough milk to make one and one-half cups liquid. Add oys-ters, and as soon as heated pour over toasted crackers.

Oysters

Oysters à la Creole

Clean one pint oysters, cook until plump, drain, and reserve liquor. Cook three tablespoons butter with three cloves, a bit of bay leaf, a slice each of carrot and onion, and a stalk of celery, five minutes. Add three tablespoons flour and pour on gradually one-half cup oyster liquor and one cup stewed and strained tomatoes. Reheat oysters in sauce, and add salt, pepper, a few drops Tabasco sauce, and one teaspoon finely chopped parsley. Serve on toast. The vegetables may be cooked with the tomatoes before the preparation of the dish; then the tomatoes may be strained ready for use.

LOBSTERS

'Tis very fresh and sweet, sir ;
The fish was taken but this night

BEAUMONT AND FLETCHER

VI

LOBSTERS

Buttered Lobster

REMOVE the meat from a two-pound lobster, and chop slightly. Melt three tablespoons butter, add lobster, and cook until thoroughly heated. Season with salt, paprika, and lemon juice.

Devilled Lobster

Mix one and one-half cups lobster meat, cut in dice, with two tablespoons olive oil and one tablespoon vinegar. Melt three tablespoons butter, add four tablespoons tomato catsup and the lobster dice. Season with one-half teaspoon mustard, one and one-half teaspoons lemon juice, salt, and cayenne. Serve as soon as thoroughly heated.

Sautéd Lobster

Remove tail meat from a two-pound lobster, and cut in four pieces; also remove meat from large claws. Sprinkle with salt, paprika, and lemon juice. Dip in crumbs, egg and crumbs,

55

and sauté, using enough butter to prevent burning. Lobster becomes tough if over-cooked. Serve with sauce Tartare.

Creamed Lobster

Remove the meat from a two-pound lobster, and cut in cubes. Melt three tablespoons butter, add four tablespoons flour mixed with one-half teaspoon salt and one-eighth teaspoon paprika. Pour on gradually one and one-half cups milk. As soon as sauce thickens, add lobster meat and two teaspoons lemon juice. Serve with brown bread or Graham bread sandwiches.

Curried Lobster, I

Prepare same as Creamed Lobster, adding one teaspoon curry powder to flour when making sauce.

Curried Lobster, II

Remove the meat from a two-pound lobster and cut in cubes. Cook three tablespoons butter with one-half tablespoon finely chopped onion until yellow. Add three tablespoons flour mixed with one-half tablespoon curry powder, one-half teaspoon salt, and one-eighth teaspoon paprika. Pour on gradually two cups milk. Mash the yolks of three hard-boiled

Lobsters

eggs, and mix with the liver of the lobster. Add lobster cubes to sauce, and, as soon as heated, the egg mixture. Serve with boiled rice.

Fricassee of Lobster

Remove the meat from a two-pound lobster, and chop. Add the yolks of three hard-boiled eggs rubbed to a paste, one-half teaspoon finely chopped parsley, one-half teaspoon salt, one-eighth teaspoon paprika, and a slight grating nutmeg. Melt three tablespoons butter, add four tablespoons flour, and pour on gradually one and one-half cups milk. Heat lobster with seasonings in sauce. Serve with saltines.

Lobster à la Béchamel

Remove the meat from a two-pound lobster, and cut in cubes. Scald two cups milk with one-half slice onion and a bit of bay leaf; remove seasonings. Melt three tablespoons butter, add four tablespoons flour mixed with one-half teaspoon salt, a few grains cayenne, and a slight grating nutmeg. Pour on gradually the scalded milk. Heat lobster in sauce, add the yolks of two eggs slightly beaten, one and one-half teaspoons lemon juice and one teaspoon parsley finely chopped.

Chafing Dish Possibilities

Lobster à la Poulette

Remove the meat from a two-pound lobster, and cut in cubes. Season with salt, paprika, and lemon juice. Melt three tablespoons butter, add three tablespoons flour, mixed with one half teaspoon salt, and pour on gradually three-fourths cup highly seasoned chicken stock. Add lobster meat, and, as soon as heated, three-fourths cup cream. Have ready the yolks of two hard-boiled eggs and the lobster coral forced through a potato ricer. Serve lobster on zephyrettes, and sprinkle with egg and coral.

Lobster à la Américaine

Cook two tablespoons butter with one-half tablespoon finely chopped onion, until yellow. Add two tablespoons flour and pour on gradually one cup stewed and strained tomatoes. To lobster liver add one tablespoon sherry wine and add to sauce. Season with one-half teaspoon salt and one-eighth teaspoon paprika. Add one and one-half cups lobster meat cut in dice. As soon as heated, add one tablespoon sherry wine.

Lobster à la Delmonico

Melt one-fourth cup butter, add one table-spoon flour, one-half teaspoon salt, a few grains

58

Lobsters

cayenne, and a slight grating of nutmeg. Pour on gradually one cup thin cream. Add the meat from a two-pound lobster cut in dice, and when heated add the yolks of two eggs and two tablespoons sherry wine.

Lobster à la Newburg

Remove the meat from a two-pound lobster, and cut in slices or cubes. Melt one-fourth cup butter, add the lobster, and cook until thoroughly heated. Season with one-half teaspoon salt, a few grains cayenne, a slight grating nutmeg, and one tablespoon each sherry wine and brandy. Cook one minute, and add one-third cup thin cream and the yolks of two eggs slightly beaten. Stir until sauce is thickened. Serve with toast or puff paste points.

Lobster and Mushroom Fricassee

Cook one cup mushrooms, cleaned and broken in pieces, in one-fourth cup butter, with a few drops onion juice, three minutes. Add one-fourth cup flour, mixed with one-half teaspoon salt and one-eighth teaspoon paprika, and one and one-half cups milk. Reheat one and one-half cups lobster meat cut in dice in the sauce. Just before serving add two tablespoons sherry wine.

SOME OTHER SHELL-FISH

Variety's the very spice of life
That gives it all its flavor

                    COWPER

VII

Clams à la Newburg

CLEAN one pint clams, remove soft parts, and finely chop hard parts. Melt three tablespoons butter, add chopped clams, one-half teaspoon salt, a few grains cayenne, and three tablespoons sherry wine. Cook eight minutes ; add soft part of clams and one-half cup thin cream. Cook two minutes, then add yolks of three eggs, slightly beaten, diluted with some of the hot sauce.

Creamed Crabs

Remove the meat from one dozen hard-shelled crabs. Cook four tablespoons butter with one-half shallot, finely chopped, until yellow; add four tablespoons flour, and pour on gradually two cups cream. Add crab meat, one-half teaspoon salt, one-fourth teaspoon paprika, a slight grating nutmeg, and two table-spoons sherry wine.

Chafing Dish Possibilities

Devilled Crabs

Melt two tablespoons butter, add two tablespoons flour, and pour on gradually one and one-fourth cups chicken stock. As soon as mixture thickens, add one cup crab meat, one-fourth cup finely chopped mushrooms, one-half teaspoon salt, one-fourth teaspoon paprika, two tablespoons sherry wine, yolks of two eggs, and one teaspoon finely chopped parsley. Serve with saltines.

Crabs à la Richmond

Cook one cup crab meat in one teaspoon butter and two tablespoons sherry wine, two minutes. Melt two tablespoons butter, add two tablespoons flour, and pour on gradually one-third cup milk and one-third cup clam broth. Add crab meat and the soft part of eighteen clams to sauce. When thoroughly heated, season with salt and paprika. Just before serving add one tablespoon brandy and the yolk of one egg, slightly beaten.

Stewed Scallops

Clean and cut in halves one pint scallops. Cook in chafing dish until liquor flows freely. Avoid cooking too long, for by so doing scallops become tough. Strain liquor, add two cups milk, and, as soon as heated, scallops. Season with two tablespoons butter, salt and pepper. Serve with small crackers.

Devilled Scallops

Clean one pint scallops, heat to boiling point, drain, and reserve liquor. Melt three table-spoons butter, add two tablespoons flour, mixed with one-half teaspoon salt, one-fourth teaspoon mustard, and a few grains cayenne. Pour on gradually the reserved liquor. When sauce begins to thicken, add the scallops. Serve with brown bread sandwiches.

Fried Scallops

Cook one pint selected scallops in blazer, until liquor flows freely from them. Drain, and dry on a towel. Sprinkle with salt and pepper, dip in crumbs, egg and crumbs, and fry in a small quantity of hot fat, being careful to do but few at a time. Serve with mayonnaise dressing or sauce Tartare.

Shrimps with Curried Rice

Cook three tablespoons butter with one-half tablespoon finely chopped onion, until yellow; then add one and one-half tablespoons corn-starch mixed with two teaspoons curry powder,

Chafing Dish Possibilities

one teaspoon salt, and one-eighth teaspoon paprika. Pour on gradually two cups milk, then add one and one-half cups shrimps, broken in pieces, and one cup warm, boiled rice.

Shrimp Wiggle

Melt four tablespoons butter, and add three tablespoons flour mixed with one-half teaspoon salt and one-eighth teaspoon pepper. Pour on gradually one and one-half cups milk. As soon as sauce thickens, add one cup shrimps, broken in pieces, and one cup canned peas, drained from their liquor and thoroughly rinsed.

Creamed Shrimps with Mushrooms

Melt three tablespoons butter, and add three tablespoons flour mixed with one-half teaspoon salt and a few grains paprika. Pour on gradually one and one-half cups milk. As soon as mixture thickens, add one cup shrimps, broken in pieces, and one-half cup canned mushrooms cut in quarters.

Shrimps à la Béchamel

Cook three tablespoons butter with one-half tablespoon finely chopped onion, five minutes, add three tablespoons flour, and pour on grad-

Some Other Shell-Fish

ually three-fourths cup each highly seasoned chicken stock and milk. Add one and one-half cups shrimps, broken in pieces, and when thoroughly heated the yolks of two eggs, slightly beaten.

Devilled Shrimps

Cook two tablespoons butter with one-half shallot, finely chopped, five minutes. Cream two tablespoons butter, add four tablespoons flour and the yolks of three hard-boiled eggs rubbed to a paste. Add to melted butter, and when well mixed pour on gradually two cups milk. Add one can shrimps, broken in pieces, one-half teaspoon salt, one-fourth teaspoon mustard, and one-eighth teaspoon pepper. Serve with puff paste points or Graham toast.

Shrimps in Tomato Sauce

Fry one small onion in three tablespoons butter, until yellow; add three tablespoons flour and stir until mixture is smooth. Pour on gradually one and one-half cups stewed and strained tomatoes, and add one can shrimps, rinsed, drained, cleaned, and broken in pieces. Season with one-half teaspoon salt and one-eighth teaspoon paprika. Serve as soon as shrimps are heated.

FISH RECHAUFFES

This dish of meat is too good for any but anglers or very honest men

WALTON

VIII

Creamed Salmon

MELT two tablespoons butter, add two table-spoons flour mixed with one-half teaspoon salt, and a few grains cayenne. Pour on gradually three-fourths cup milk. Add one cup canned salmon, drained and flaked. Just before serv-ing add yolks of two eggs, slightly beaten, and a slight grating of nutmeg.

Sautéd Fillets of Salmon

Sprinkle small slices of salmon with salt and pepper; sauté in a hot blazer, using enough butter to prevent burning. Season with lemon juice and sprinkle with finely chopped parsley.

Fish à la Provençale

Melt one-fourth cup butter, add two and one-half tablespoons flour, and pour on gradually two cups milk. Mash yolks of four hard-boiled eggs, and mix with one teaspoon anchovy essence, add to sauce, then add two cups cold boiled, flaked fish.

Creamed Salt Codfish

Pick in pieces and soak in lukewarm water one and one-half cups fish; drain as soon as soft. Melt three tablespoons butter, add two tablespoons flour and a few grains pepper. Pour on gradually one and one-half cups milk. Add fish and one egg, slightly beaten. Pour over slices of toasted bread, covered with slices of hard-boiled eggs.

Salt Codfish with Cheese

Prepare codfish as in preceding recipe. Melt two tablespoons butter, add one and one-half tablespoons flour mixed with one-eighth teaspoon paprika, and pour on gradually one cup milk. Add fish and one-half cup grated cheese. As soon as cheese is melted, add one egg, slightly beaten.

Grilled Sardines

Drain twelve sardines and cook until heated, turning frequently. Arrange on small oblong pieces of dry toast and serve with Maître d'Hôtel butter.

Fish Réchauffés

Ragoût of Sardines, I

Drain sardines, remove backbones, and separate in pieces. Heat in blazer, season with salt and paprika, and add sherry wine to moisten. Serve on zephyrettes.

Ragoût of Sardines, II

Drain sardines, remove backbones, and separate in pieces. Heat in blazer, using enough butter to moisten. Season with Worcestershire sauce and cayenne, allowing one teaspoon sauce and one-eighth teaspoon cayenne for twelve fish.

Sardines with Anchovy Sauce

Drain twelve sardines and cook until heated, turning frequently. Make one cup brown sauce with one and one-half tablespoons sardine oil, two tablespoons flour, one cup brown stock, and anchovy essence to taste. Reheat sardines in sauce. Serve with brown bread sandwiches.

Sardines à la Hollandaise

Drain twelve sardines, heat and arrange on oblong pieces of toast. Melt two tablespoons butter, add one-half tablespoon Chutney, one-fourth teaspoon salt, one-eighth teaspoon

Chafing Dish Possibilities

paprika, the yolks of two eggs, and one-half tablespoon lemon juice. Stir constantly until sauce begins to thicken, then add two tablespoons butter and one-fourth cup boiling water. Pour sauce over sardines.

Devilled Sardines

Drain twelve sardines, and cook until heated. Mix two tablespoons sardine oil, one-half tablespoon Worcestershire sauce, one-half tablespoon vinegar, one teaspoon lemon juice, one-fourth teaspoon salt, and one-eighth teaspoon paprika. Heat and pour over sardines.

BEEF

The empty spit
Ne'er cherished wit:
Minerva loves the larder

W. CARTWRIGHT

IX

Warmed Over Beef

MELT two tablespoons butter, add two table-spoons flour, and pour on gradually one-half cup stewed and strained tomatoes and one-fourth cup stock or water. Season with one-half tea-spoon salt, one-eighth teaspoon paprika, and a few drops onion juice. Add one cup rare chopped beef; cook one minute, and serve.

Réchauffé of Beef

Brown two tablespoons butter, add three tablespoons flour, and, when well browned, pour on gradually one cup stock. Season with one-fourth teaspoon salt, one-eighth teaspoon paprika, a few grains each of mustard and curry powder, and two tablespoons sherry wine. Pour sauce over thin slices of rare roast beef.

Beef Balls

Cut one-half pound beef from top of round, in one-third inch strips, and scrape with a rather dull knife. Remove all soft part of beef from

77

Chafing Dish Possibilities

freshly cut side; turn, and scrape other side. Season with salt and pepper, and shape into small balls, about the size of filberts, using as little pressure as possible. Drop balls into a hot blazer, generously sprinkled with salt, shaking pan constantly until the entire surface of the balls is seared. Serve on oblong pieces of buttered toast.

Cecils, I

Brown one and one-half tablespoons butter, add three tablespoons flour, and pour on gradually one-half cup milk. Then add one cup raw beef, finely chopped, one-half teaspoon lemon juice, a few drops onion juice, and salt and pepper. Chill mixture, shape in small cakes, dip in crumbs; egg and crumbs, and sauté in hot blaz r, using enough butter to prevent burning.

Cecils, II

Season one cup rare roast beef, finely chopped, with salt, pepper, onion juice, and Worcestershire sauce. Add two tablespoons stale breadcrumbs, one tablespoon melted butter, and one egg yolk, slightly beaten. Shape into very small croquettes, roll in flour, egg and crumbs, and sauté in hot blazer, turning often, and using enough butter to prevent burning.

Beef

Hamburg Steaks

Chop finely one-half pound lean, raw beef, and season highly with salt, pepper, and onion juice. Shape into small steaks, using as little pressure as possible. Put into a hot buttered blazer; sear on one side, turn and sear other side. Cook five minutes, turning frequently. Spread with one and one-half tablespoons butter, which has been creamed and mixed with one-fourth teaspoon salt and a few grains pepper.

Vienna Steaks

Chop one-fourth pound each of raw, lean beef and veal, taking care to remove all fat and membrane. Season with three-fourths teaspoon salt, one-fourth teaspoon each paprika and celery salt, a few gratings nutmeg, one teaspoon lemon juice, and a few drops onion juice. Add one egg, well beaten, let stand several hours, then shape into small steaks. Put into a hot, buttered blazer, sear on one side, turn and sear other side. Cook six to eight minutes, turning frequently. Cream one and one-half tablespoons butter, mix with one-fourth teaspoon salt and a few grains pepper. Spread on steaks.

Chafing Dish Possibilities

Broiled Fillet of Beef

Put slices of tenderloin steak, cut three-fourths inch thick, into a hot blazer which has been rubbed over with a piece of beef fat. Sear on one side, turn and sear other side. Cook four minutes, turning frequently. Spread with soft butter, and sprinkle with salt and pepper.

Broiled Fillet of Beef with Horse-radish Sauce

Serve broiled fillet of beef with horse-radish sauce.

Horse-radish Sauce

Beat four tablespoons heavy cream until stiff, add three tablespoons grated horse-radish root, mixed with one tablespoon vinegar, one-fourth teaspoon salt, and a few grains cayenne.

Broiled Steaks à la Creole

Broil tenderloin steaks and serve with Creole sauce.

Creole Sauce

Cook two tablespoons butter with two tablespoons onion and four tablespoons green pepper, both finely chopped, five minutes. Add one and one-half cups canned tomatoes, drained

Beef

from their liquor, and six olives from which the stones have been removed; then add one cup brown sauce, which has been prepared previously. Bring to boiling point, and add salt, pepper, and sherry wine.

Dried Beef with Cream Sauce

Remove skin from one-fourth pound smoked, dried beef; separate in pieces, cover with hot water, let stand ten minutes, and drain. Melt two tablespoons butter, add one and one-half tablespoons flour, and pour on gradually one cup milk. Season with salt and pepper. Reheat beef in sauce, and pour over strips of toasted bread. If preferred richer, add the yolk of one egg just before serving.

Hash Balls

Chop cold cooked, corned beef from which the skin, gristle, and most of the fat have been removed. Add an equal quantity of cold boiled potatoes, chopped and seasoned with salt, pepper, and onion juice. Moisten with milk or cream, make into small flat cakes, and cook in a hot buttered blazer. Brown on one side, turn, and brown other side.

LAMB AND MUTTON

" A little pot is soon hot "

X

LAMB AND MUTTON

Lamb Chops, Pan Broiled

WIPE chops, and trim off superfluous fat. Rub over the blazer with some of the fat. Put chops in blazer, sear on one side, turn and sear other side. Cook from six to eight minutes, turning occasionally. Season with salt and pepper when half cooked. Drain and spread with soft butter.

Breaded Chops

Prepare chops as for Pan Broiled Chops. Sprinkle with salt and pepper, dip in crumbs, egg and crumbs, and sauté from six to eight minutes in a small quantity of hot fat. Serve with tomato sauce.

Hashed Mutton

Cook two tablespoons butter with one tablespoon finely chopped onion, five minutes. Add two tablespoons flour and pour on gradually

85

Chafing Dish Possibilities

one cup stock. Add one cup cold chopped, cooked mutton, one-half cup cold boiled potatoes, cut in dice, and one tomato, skinned and cut in small pieces. Season with salt, pepper, and celery salt; cover and cook over hot water, ten minutes.

Minced Lamb

Chop remnants of cold roast lamb; there should be one cup. Put two tablespoons butter in hot blazer, add lamb, sprinkle with salt, pepper, and celery salt, and dredge thoroughly with flour; then add enough stock or water to moisten. Serve on small slices of buttered toast.

Lamb Collops with Tomato Sauce

Take small, thick pieces of roast lamb or boiled mutton. Sprinkle with salt and pepper, dip in crumbs, egg and crumbs, and sauté in a hot blazer, using enough butter to prevent burning. Serve with tomato sauce.

Blanquette of Lamb

Melt three tablespoons butter, add three tablespoons flour, and pour on gradually two-thirds cup each milk and white stock. Season with salt, pepper, and three-fourths tablespoon

Lamb and Mutton

mushroom catsup. Cut cold roast lamb in strips or cubes (there should be one and one-half cups) and reheat in sauce. Serve with entire wheat bread sandwiches.

Mutton Ragoût

Beat currant jelly, that it may be easily measured. Put three tablespoons jelly in hot blazer, add one teaspoon lemon juice and two tablespoons butter. When butter is melted, reheat thin slices of cold boiled mutton in sauce. Season with salt and paprika.

Mock Terrapin

Mash the yolks of three hard-boiled eggs, and season with one-half teaspoon salt, one-half teaspoon mixed mustard, and one-eighth teaspoon paprika. Add one cup chopped, cooked mutton and one-half cup cream. Put into a hot blazer, and when thoroughly heated add two tablespoons sherry wine. Serve on toast.

Mutton with Currant Jelly Sauce

Brown two tablespoons butter, add three tablespoons flour mixed with one-fourth teaspoon salt and one-eighth teaspoon paprika, and when well browned pour on gradually one cup brown stock. Add one-third cup currant jelly and six slices of cold cooked mutton. When meat is heated, add one and one-half tablespoons sherry wine.

Lamb, Sauce Piquante

Cook three tablespoons butter with one-half shallot, finely chopped, five minutes. Add four tablespoons flour, and pour on gradually one and one-half cups brown stock. Add one-half teaspoon salt, one-eighth teaspoon paprika, one-half tablespoon vinegar, one tablespoon capers, and six sliced, canned mushrooms. Reheat slices of cold cooked mutton in sauce.

Salmi of Lamb

Cook two tablespoons butter, with one-half tablespoon finely chopped onion, five minutes. Add three tablespoons flour, and cook until well browned, then pour on gradually one cup brown stock. Season with one-fourth teaspoon salt, one-eighth teaspoon pepper, and one teaspoon Worcestershire, Harvey, or Elizabeth sauce. Reheat slices of cold roast lamb in sauce. This dish is greatly improved by the addition of one-third cup mushrooms, cut in quarters, or ten olives from which the stones have been removed.

CHICKEN

There's no want of meat, sir;
Portly and curious viands are prepared,
To please all kinds of appetite

                                        MASSINGER

XI

CHICKEN

Creamed Chicken and Peas

MELT four tablespoons butter, add five table-spoons flour, mixed with one-fourth teaspoon salt and one-eighth teaspoon pepper. Pour on gradually one and three-fourths cups milk. When sauce thickens, add one and one-half cups cold boiled fowl, cut in dice, and two-thirds cup canned peas, drained and rinsed.

Chicken and Oysters, à la Métropole

Melt four tablespoons butter, and add four tablespoons flour, mixed with one-half teaspoon salt and one-eighth teaspoon pepper. Pour on gradually one and three-fourths cups milk, then add two cups cold boiled fowl, cut in dice, and one pint oysters, cleaned and drained. Cook until oysters are plump. Serve on zephyrettes, and sprinkle with finely chopped celery.

Chicken Hollandaise

Cook three tablespoons butter with one tea-spoon finely chopped onion, until yellow; add

Chafing Dish Possibilities

one tablespoon cornstarch, and pour on gradu
ally one and one-half cups chicken stock. Stir
until mixture thickens slightly, then add one-
half tablespoon lemon juice, three-fourths teaspoon salt, one-eighth teaspoon paprika, one-half
cup finely chopped celery, and one and one-
half cups chopped, cooked chicken. When
thoroughly heated, add the beaten yolks of two
eggs, and cook one minute. Serve with buttered
Graham toast.

Chicken with Tomatoes

Cook four tablespoons butter, with one-half
shallot, finely chopped, five minutes. Add five
tablespoons flour, and stir until slightly browned.
Pour on gradually three-fourths cup each
chicken stock and stewed and strained tomatoes. Add one teaspoon lemon juice, one-half
teaspoon salt, and one-eighth teaspoon paprika.
Reheat one and one-half cups cold boiled fowl,
cut in cubes in the sauce.

Chicken à la Reine

Cream two tablespoons butter and add the
yolks of three hard-boiled eggs, rubbed to a
paste. Soak one-fourth cup cracker crumbs in
one-fourth cup milk and add to the egg mixture. Pour on gradually one cup hot chicken

Chicken

stock, then add one cup cooked chicken, finely cut. Season with salt, paprika, and celery salt. Serve on toast.

Minced Chicken with Green Peppers

Boil two green peppers ten minutes, remove seeds, and cut in small strips. Mix with two cups cold cooked fowl, cut in dice. Melt three tablespoons butter, add three tablespoons flour, and pour on gradually one and one-third cups chicken stock. Add chicken and peppers. Season with salt and pepper, and serve on circular pieces of toast.

Devilled Bones

Melt two tablespoons butter, add one tablespoon each Chili sauce, Worcestershire sauce, and walnut catsup, one teaspoon made mustard, and a few grains cayenne. Cut four small gashes in the drumsticks, second joints, and wings of a cooked chicken. Sprinkle with salt and pepper, dredge with flour, and cook in the seasoned butter until well browned. Add one-half cup stock, simmer five minutes, and sprinkle with finely chopped parsley.

India Curry

Melt two tablespoons butter, and add the breast and second joints of a cooked chicken

Chafing Dish Possibilities

cut in small pieces. When chicken is thoroughly heated remove, and in the same dish make the following sauce. Cook two tablespoons butter with one-half small onion, finely chopped, one clove garlic, finely chopped, and three-fourths teaspoon grated ginger root, five minutes. Add two tablespoons cornstarch mixed with one tablespoon curry powder. Grate a cocoanut and add two cups milk, let stand one hour, and drain through cheese-cloth. Add milk thus obtained to butter and cornstarch mixture to complete sauce. Reheat chicken in sauce. Cocoanuts often may be bought of a caterer, who will prepare them as desired. One is well repaid for the time spent in preparing this dish.

Sautéd Chickens' Livers

Cut one slice bacon in small pieces, and cook with two tablespoons butter, five minutes. Remove bacon, add one shallot, finely chopped, and fry five minutes; then add six chickens' livers cleaned and separated, and cook five minutes. Add two tablespoons flour, mix thoroughly, then add one cup brown stock, one teaspoon lemon juice, and one-fourth cup sliced mushrooms. Cook two minutes, and sprinkle with finely chopped parsley. In cleaning livers carefully remove gall bladder.

Chicken

Chickens' Livers with Curry

Clean and separate six chickens' livers. Dip in seasoned crumbs, egg and crumbs, and sauté in butter. Remove livers, and to fat in blazer add two tablespoons butter and one-half tablespoon finely chopped onion; cook five minutes. Add three tablespoons flour mixed with one-half teaspoon curry powder, one-fourth teaspoon salt, and one-eighth teaspoon paprika. Strain sauce over livers.

Chickens' Livers with Tomato Sauce

Sauté chickens' livers, and serve with tomato sauce.

Tomato Sauce

Brown two tablespoons butter with one-half tablespoon finely chopped onion, two cloves, a bit of bay leaf, and a sprig of parsley. Add three tablespoons flour and continue browning. Pour on gradually one-half cup each stock and stewed and strained tomatoes. Season with salt, pepper, and a few grains of cayenne. Strain before serving.

Chickens' Livers with Bacon

Clean livers, separate into six pieces, and sprinkle with salt and pepper. Wrap each piece separately in a thin slice of bacon and fasten with a small wooden skewer. Put into a hot blazer and cook until bacon is brown, turning frequently and removing some of the fat if necessary.

Chickens' Livers with Madeira Sauce

Clean and separate livers, sprinkle with salt and pepper, dredge with flour, and sauté in butter. Brown two tablespoons butter, add three tablespoons flour, and when well browned pour on gradually one cup brown stock. Season with salt and pepper. Reheat livers in sauce, and add two tablespoons Madeira wine.

Chickens' Livers with Olive Sauce

Prepare livers same as Chickens' Livers with Madeira Sauce. Brown two tablespoons butter, add three tablespoons flour, and when well browned pour on gradually one cup highly seasoned brown stock. Season with salt and pepper, add twelve olives, from which the stones have been removed, and cook three minutes. Pour around livers.

SWEETBREADS

Not to know me argues yourself unknown

MILTON

XII

SWEETBREADS

Creamed Sweetbreads

REMOVE tubes and membrane from one pair sweetbreads, clean and parboil in boiling, salted, acidulated water, twenty minutes; allowing one-half tablespoon each salt, and vinegar or lemon juice, to each pair sweetbreads. Drain and plunge into cold water; as soon as cool, remove from water and cut in one-half inch cubes. Melt two tablespoons butter, add two and one-half tablespoons flour, mixed with one-fourth teaspoon salt and a few grains of pepper. Pour on gradually one cup milk, then reheat sweetbreads in sauce.

Creamed Sweetbreads and Chicken

Prepare same as Creamed Sweetbreads, using equal parts of cold cooked chicken, cut in dice, and sweetbreads, cut in dice.

99

Chafing Dish Possibilities

Sweetbreads à la Poulette

Melt two tablespoons butter, add two tablespoons flour, and pour on gradually one-half cup each chicken stock and milk. Reheat sweetbreads, cut in dice, in sauce. Season with salt and pepper, and just before serving add the yolks of two eggs and a slight grating of nutmeg.

Sweetbreads with Mushrooms

Parboil one pair sweetbreads and cut in dice. Cook two tablespoons chopped mushrooms in three tablespoons butter, five minutes. Add two and one-half tablespoons flour, mixed with one-half teaspoon salt and one-eighth teaspoon paprika, and pour on gradually one cup milk and one-fourth cup mushroom liquor. Add the sweetbread dice and one teaspoon lemon juice. Just before serving, add the yolks of two eggs and one teaspoon finely chopped parsley.

Sweetbreads with Peas

Parboil one pair sweetbreads and cut in cubes. Drain three-fourths cup canned peas from their liquor, rinse, and add to sweetbreads. Melt three tablespoons butter, add three tablespoons flour, mixed with three-fourths teaspoon salt and one-eighth teaspoon paprika. Pour on

Sweetbreads

gradually one cup milk. Reheat sweetbreads and peas in sauce, and just before serving add one-half cup cream.

Sweetbreads, Spanish Style

Parboil one pair sweetbreads, and cut in slices. Cook two tablespoons butter, with one-half shallot finely chopped, one-fourth green pepper, freed from seeds and finely chopped, and two tomatoes, skinned and cut in pieces, ten minutes. Add one cup cold boiled potatoes, cut in cubes, and the sweetbreads. Season with salt and pepper.

Sweetbreads and Bacon

Cut thin slices of bacon in strips. Put into a hot blazer, and fry until brown. Remove bacon, and use fat in pan for sautéing sweetbreads. Parboil sweetbreads, and cut in one-third inch slices. Sprinkle with salt and pepper, dip in crumbs, egg and crumbs, and sauté until delicately browned. Drain and serve with bacon.

Sweetbreads with Tomato Sauce

Parboil sweetbreads, cut in one-third inch slices, and dip in crumbs, egg and crumbs. Put into a hot, buttered blazer, and sauté until delicately browned, using enough butter to prevent burning. Serve with Tomato Sauce.

Chafing Dish Possibilities

Tomato Sauce

Cook one cup canned tomatoes with one teaspoon sugar, one-eighth teaspoon pepper, and a bit of bay leaf, five minutes. Strain and add one-half cup brown stock. Brown two tablespoons butter, add three tablespoons flour, and pour on gradually the liquid. Season with salt.

Sweetbreads with Asparagus Tips

Prepare and sauté one pair sweetbreads. Melt two tablespoons butter, add two tablespoons flour mixed with one-fourth teaspoon salt and a few grains of pepper. Pour on gradually one cup milk, then add one cup asparagus tips, rinsed and drained. Pour around sweetbreads just before serving.

Sweetbreads, Olive Sauce

Prepare and sauté one pair sweetbreads. Cook two tablespoons butter with one teaspoon finely chopped onion, until slightly browned. Add three tablespoons flour, and cook until well browned. Pour on gradually one cup brown stock, then add one dozen olives from which the stones have been removed. Cook three minutes, season with salt and pepper, and pour around sweetbreads.

WITH THE EPICURE

Not all on books their criticism waste :
The genius of a dish some justly taste,
And eat their way to fame

                                          YOUNG

XIII

WITH THE EPICURE

Stewed Frogs' Legs

CLEAN and trim one dozen frogs' hind legs.
Melt two and one-half tablespoons butter, add
frogs' legs, and cook five minutes. Dredge
with two tablespoons flour, and pour on gradually three-fourths cup chicken stock; cover,
and simmer twelve minutes. Add one-fourth
cup cream, and season with salt and pepper.

Fried Frogs' Legs

Clean and trim one dozen frogs' hind legs.
Season with salt and pepper, roll in crumbs,
egg and crumbs, and sauté in a hot blazer, using
enough butter to prevent burning. Do not
attempt to cook too many at a time, as they
should be well browned. Serve with Sauce
Tartare.

Stewed Lambs' Kidneys

Soak in cold water, pare, remove fat from
centres, and cut in slices six kidneys; sprinkle

Chafing Dish Possibilities

with salt and pepper. Melt two tablespoons butter, add kidneys, and cook eight minutes. Dredge thoroughly with flour, pour on gradually two-thirds cup water or brown stock, and cook six minutes. Season with salt, pepper, a few drops onion juice and Worcestershire sauce.

Lambs' Kidneys, Madeira Sauce

Prepare kidneys as for stewed kidneys. Sprinkle with salt and pepper, roll in flour, and sauté in a hot blazer, using enough butter to prevent burning. Cook two tablespoons butter with one-half tablespoon finely chopped onion, until slightly browned; add four tablespoons flour, and cook until well browned; then pour on gradually one and one-half cups brown stock. Season with salt and pepper, strain, add kidneys and one tablespoon Madeira wine.

Kidney Toast

Soak in cold water, pare, remove fat from centres, and chop four lambs' kidneys. Cook three tablespoons butter with one-half tablespoon finely chopped onion and one teaspoon finely chopped parsley, five minutes. Add kidneys, and season with salt, pepper, one-half tablespoon Worcestershire sauce, and one tea-

spoon lemon juice. Dredge with one tablespoon flour, stir until well mixed, and add
gradually one-half cup stock. When thoroughly
heated add four tablespoons grated cheese, and
as soon as cheese has melted serve on pieces of
toast.

Calf's Brains with Scrambled Eggs

Prepare brains for subsequent cooking same
as sweetbreads are prepared, then separate into
pieces. Add to scrambled eggs.

Calf's Brains, Vinaigrette Sauce

Prepare brains same as sweetbreads, reheat
in boiling water, drain, and separate into pieces.
Mix three tablespoons olive oil, one tablespoon
vinegar, one teaspoon each grated onion,
chopped parsley, and chopped capers, and
one-fourth teaspoon each salt and pepper.
Pour sauce over brains.

Fried Calf's Brains, Sauce Tartare

Prepare brains same as sweetbreads, and cut
in four pieces. Sprinkle with salt and pepper,
roll in flour, dip in egg and stale bread crumbs,
and sauté, using enough butter to prevent burning. Serve with Sauce Tartare.

Chafing Dish Possibilities

Tripe in Batter

Wipe tripe and cut in pieces for serving, sprinkle with salt and pepper and dip in batter made of one cup flour, one-fourth teaspoon salt, one-half cup cold water, one egg well beaten, and one teaspoon olive oil or melted butter. Sauté in a small quantity of hot fat. In tripe recipes use fresh honeycomb tripe, unless otherwise specified.

Fried Tripe

Wipe tripe and cut in pieces for serving. Sprinkle with salt and pepper, dip in flour, egg, and crumbs, and sauté in a small quantity of hot fat until delicately browned.

Tripe with Bacon

Cut slices of bacon in strips, and fry until crisp ; then remove bacon. Wipe pickled tripe and cut in pieces for serving. Sprinkle with salt and pepper, roll in corn meal, and sauté in bacon fat. Serve with the crisp bacon.

Lyonnaise Tripe

Wipe tripe and cut in pieces two inches long by one and one-half inches wide; there should be three cups. Put in blazer, cover, let stand one minute, that some of the moisture may be withdrawn, and drain. Cook two tablespoons butter with one tablespoon finely chopped onion, until yellow, add tripe and cook eight minutes, using more butter if necessary. Season with salt and pepper, and sprinkle with finely chopped parsley.

Tripe à la Provençale

To Lyonnaise Tripe from which the parsley has been omitted, add one tablespoon white wine. Cook until quite dry, then add one-half cup tomato sauce.

Tripe à la Creole

Cut tripe in pieces as for Lyonnaise Tripe. Cook two tablespoons butter with one tablespoon finely chopped onion and one-eighth green pepper, finely chopped, five minutes. Add one tablespoon flour, one-half cup stock, one-fourth cup drained tomatoes, and one fresh mushroom, cut in slices. Add tripe and cook eight minutes. Season with salt and pepper.

Tripe à la Bordelaise

Prepare tripe as for Lyonnaise Tripe. Cook two tablespoons butter with one tablespoon chopped onion, five minutes. Add tripe and

109

cook until slightly browned. Season with salt and pepper, and add one teaspoon finely chopped parsley. Serve with sliced tomatoes.

Curried Tripe

Prepare tripe as for Lyonnaise Tripe. Cook three tablespoons butter with one tablespoon finely chopped onion, five minutes. Add two tablespoons flour mixed with two teaspoons curry powder, and one-fourth teaspoon salt. Pour on gradually three-fourths cup cream, add the tripe, and cook eight minutes.

Shad Roe, Tomato Sauce

Cook shad roe in boiling, salted, acidulated water, fifteen minutes. Drain, cover with cold water, let stand five minutes, again drain, and dry in a piece of cheese-cloth. Sprinkle with salt and pepper, roll in flour, egg and crumbs, and sauté in butter. Serve with Tomato Sauce.

Shad Roe with Bacon

Trim six slices of bacon, put into a hot blazer, and cook until well browned. Cook shad roe as for Shad Roe with Tomato Sauce. Rub the yolks of two hard-boiled eggs to a paste, add one-half teaspoon mustard, one-fourth teaspoon salt, one-eighth teaspoon paprika, three-fourths teaspoon lemon juice, and enough thick cream to moisten. Spread roe with mixture, roll in flour, egg and crumbs, and sauté in bacon fat. Serve with the bacon.

Ragoût of Shad Roe

Clean a shad roe and parboil in boiling, salted, acidulated water, to which has been added a slice of onion, a sprig of parsley, and a bit of bay leaf. Drain, and plunge into cold water; remove membrane and separate roe in pieces. Melt three tablespoons butter, add roe, and, when thoroughly heated, one-third cup cream. Season with salt and pepper and just before serving add the yolks of two eggs slightly beaten; if preferred more highly seasoned, add one tablespoon lemon juice, one table-spoon sherry wine, and a slight grating nutmeg.

Mackerel Roe with Maître d'Hôtel Butter

Prepare and cook mackerel roe same as shad roe. Serve with Maître d'Hôtel Butter.

Maître d'Hôtel Butter

Cream one-fourth cup butter, add one-half teaspoon salt, one-eighth teaspoon pepper, and very slowly one-fourth tablespoon lemon juice; then add one-half tablespoon finely chopped parsley.

Mackerel Roe, Egg Sauce

Sauté two mackerel roes. Melt two tablespoons butter, add two tablespoons flour, and pour on gradually one cup milk. Season with one-fourth teaspoon salt, a few grains cayenne, one teaspoon lemon juice, and just before serving add the yolks of two eggs slightly beaten. Pour over roes.

Venison Steak

Remove fat and trim slices of venison. Sprinkle with salt and pepper, and put into a hot, slightly buttered blazer. Sear on one side, turn and sear other side. Cook four minutes, turning frequently. Spread with Maître d'Hôtel Butter.

Venison Steak with Currant Jelly

Cook venison steak and remove from blazer. Melt one and one-half tablespoons butter, add a few grains paprika and two tablespoons currant jelly, and as soon as jelly has melted pour sauce over steak.

With the Epicure

Venison Cutlets with Apples

Wipe, core, and cut in one-half inch slices four sour apples. Sprinkle with powdered sugar and cover with port wine; let stand one hour, drain, and sauté in butter. Cut venison steak in pieces for serving, sprinkle with salt and pepper, and cook in a hot, buttered blazer, four minutes. Melt three tablespoons butter, add wine drained from apples and twelve candied cherries cut in halves. Reheat cutlets in sauce, and serve with apples.

Frankfort Sausages

Cook four sausages in boiling water to cover, twenty minutes; drain and cut in pieces. Reheat in a white sauce made of one and one-half tablespoons each flour and butter and one cup milk. Season with salt and pepper.

Fried Sausages

Cut large sausages in one-fourth inch slices, put into a hot blazer, and cook until heated and slightly browned on both sides. Spread with Horse-radish Mustard and serve on circular pieces of toast.

Chafing Dish Possibilities

Bean Rarebit

Melt two tablespoons butter, add one teaspoon salt, one-eighth teaspoon paprika, one cup cold baked beans mashed, and one-half cup milk or cream. When thoroughly heated, add one-half cup grated cheese. Serve on toast or zephyrettes.

Ragoût of Veal

Cook two and one-half tablespoons butter with one tablespoon finely chopped canned mushrooms and one teaspoon finely chopped onion, three minutes. Add three tablespoons flour and cook until browned. Pour on gradually one cup brown stock, and add one cup cold roast veal cut in cubes. Season with one-half tablespoon each Worcestershire sauce and mushroom catsup, salt and pepper.

Ragoût of Duck

Marinate pieces of cold roast duck, cut in pieces for serving with French dressing; cover and let stand one hour. Cook three tablespoons butter with one-half shallot finely chopped until brown. Add four tablespoons flour, and when well browned pour on gradually one and one-half cups brown stock. Season

with one-half teaspoon salt, a few grains cayenne, one teaspoon lemon juice, and two tablespoons tomato catsup. Reheat duck in sauce,
and add three tablespoons port wine and one-
half cup canned mushroom, sliced lengthwise.

Salmi of Grouse

Cut cold roast grouse in pieces for serving.
Melt one-fourth cup butter, add one tablespoon
finely chopped onion, a stalk of celery, two
slices carrot cut in pieces, and two tablespoons
chopped, lean raw ham. Cook until butter is
browned, then add one-fourth cup flour, and
when well browned add two cups brown stock,
a bit of bay leaf, a sprig of parsley, a blade of
mace, two cloves, one-half teaspoon salt, and
one-eighth teaspoon pepper. Cook five minutes, strain, add duck, and as soon as duck is
heated add sherry wine, stoned olives, and
mushrooms cut in quarters.

VEGETABLES

The common growth of Mother Earth
Suffices me,

                    WORDSWORTH

XIV

VEGETABLES

Hashed Potatoes

CUT fat salt pork in small cubes, try out, and remove scraps; there should be about one-third cup fat. Add two cups cold boiled potatoes, finely chopped, one-eighth teaspoon pepper, and salt if necessary. Mix potatoes thoroughly with fat; cook four minutes, stirring constantly; then let stand until browned underneath.

Lyonnaise Potatoes

Cook one and one-half tablespoons butter and one tablespoon finely chopped onion, five minutes. Melt three tablespoons butter, add two cups cold sliced boiled potatoes, season with salt and pepper, and cook until potatoes have absorbed butter. Add butter and onion, and when well mixed add one-half tablespoon finely chopped parsley.

Creamed Peas

Drain one can small peas, rinse thoroughly, cover with boiling water, boil one minute, and

Chafing Dish Possibilities

again drain. Melt three tablespoons butter, add the peas, and cook five minutes. Dredge with one tablespoon flour mixed with one teaspoon sugar; cook one minute. Add one-third cup cream, and salt and pepper to taste.

String Beans à la Maître d'Hôtel

Drain and rinse one can small French beans, and cut each bean in three pieces. Put into a hot blazer and heat thoroughly, adding just enough water or stock to prevent beans from burning. Cream two and one-half tablespoons butter, add one teaspoon lemon juice, one-fourth teaspoon salt, and one-eighth teaspoon paprika. Add prepared butter to beans and sprinkle with one teaspoon finely chopped parsley.

Smothered Tomatoes

Cut three small tomatoes in halves crosswise. Melt one and one-half tablespoons butter in hot blazer, arrange tomatoes in pan, skin side down, cover, and cook until soft. Season with salt and pepper, and sprinkle with sugar.

Tomatoes in White Sauce

Wipe and peel three tomatoes and slice crosswise. Sprinkle with salt and pepper, roll in

Vegetables

flour and heat in blazer, using enough butter to prevent burning. Tomatoes should be watched carefully and turned during heating. Melt two tablespoons butter, add two tablespoons flour mixed with one-fourth teaspoon salt, and pour on gradually one and one-third cups milk. Stir constantly until sauce thickens, then pour over tomatoes.

Devilled Tomatoes

Wipe, peel, and slice crosswise three tomatoes. Season with salt and pepper, coat with flour, and cook in a hot blazer until thoroughly heated, using enough butter to prevent burning. Cream one-fourth cup butter, add two teaspoons powdered sugar, one teaspoon mustard, one-fourth teaspoon salt, a few grains cayenne, the yolk of one hard-boiled egg, one egg slightly beaten, and two tablespoons vinegar. Cook over hot water, stirring constantly, until it thickens. Pour over tomatoes.

Tomato Curry

Cook two tablespoons butter with one-half tablespoon finely chopped onion, until yellow. Add one sour apple, pared, cored, and cut in small pieces, and cook eight minutes. Add

121

Chafing Dish Possibilities

one-half cup stock, two cups canned tomatoes, one-half tablespoon curry powder, one teaspoon vinegar, and salt and pepper to taste. As soon as boiling point is reached, add one cup boiled rice, and cook five minutes.

Curried Vegetables

Have previously prepared one cup boiled potato balls, one cup boiled carrots, cut in dice, one-half cup boiled turnips cut in dice, and one-half cup canned peas, rinsed and drained. Cook two slices onion in three tablespoons butter five minutes. Remove onion, and add three tablespoons flour, one teaspoon curry powder, one teaspoon salt, one-fourth teaspoon celery salt, one-fourth teaspoon pepper, and one and one-half cups milk. Stir until smooth, then reheat vegetables in sauce.

Corn Fritters

To one cup finely chopped canned corn add one egg, well beaten, one-fourth cup flour, and salt and pepper. Drop by small spoonfuls in a hot, well-greased blazer. Brown on one side, turn, and brown on the other. The fritters should be about the size of large oysters.

Vegetables

Corn and Celery Fritters

Prepare and cook same as Corn Fritters, substituting one-half cup finely chopped celery in place of one-half of the corn.

Rice Fritters

Wash one-half cup rice, add to one-half cup boiling water with one teaspoon salt. Cover, and steam until rice has absorbed water; then add one cup milk and steam until rice is soft. Add yolks of two eggs and one tablespoon butter. Spread in a shallow pan to cool. The steaming of the rice should be accomplished over the kitchen range. Cut in small squares, dip in crumbs, egg and crumbs, and sauté in a small quantity of hot fat. Serve with currant jelly to accompany cold meat, or as a dessert, with wine sauce.

Stewed Mushrooms

Wash one-half pound mushrooms; remove stems, scrape and cut in pieces; peel caps and break in pieces. Melt three tablespoons butter in blazer, add mushrooms, and cook four minutes. Dredge with one and one-half tablespoons flour, sprinkle with salt and pepper, add one-half cup stock, and cook eight minutes.

Chafing Dish Possibilities

Stewed Mushrooms in Cream

Prepare one-half pound mushrooms. Melt two tablespoons butter, add mushrooms, and cook four minutes. Dredge with one tablespoon flour, sprinkle with salt, paprika, and nutmeg, add three-fourths cup cream, and cook eight minutes.

Creamed Mushrooms

Prepare one-half pound mushrooms, and cook in two tablespoons butter, eight minutes. Add one and one-half tablespoons flour, and when well mixed add two-thirds cup cream. Season with salt and pepper, and when boiling point is reached add one-half tablespoon wine. Serve on toast.

Smothered Mushrooms

Prepare one-half pound mushrooms. Melt three tablespoons butter, add mushrooms, sprinkle with salt and paprika, cover and cook slowly fifteen minutes. Dredge with one and one-half tablespoons flour, and add one-half cup chicken stock. As soon as heated, add the yolks of two eggs, slightly beaten, and a slight grating nutmeg.

Sautéd Mushrooms

Prepare one-half pound mushrooms. Melt three tablespoons butter, add mushrooms, dredged with flour, a few drops onion juice, salt, and paprika; cook six minutes, then add one-third cup boiling water and cook four minutes. Sprinkle with one-teaspoon finely chopped parsley and serve on toast.

Fried Puff Balls

Clean mushrooms; remove outer skin and cut in one-half inch slices. Sprinkle with salt and pepper, dip in flour, egg, and crumbs, and fry in olive oil or clarified butter until tender and thoroughly browned.

Mushrooms à la Sabine

Prepare one-half pound mushrooms; sprinkle with salt and pepper, dredge with flour, and cook with two tablespoons butter, three minutes. Make one and one-fourth cups brown sauce, using two and one-half tablespoons butter, three tablespoons flour, and one and one-fourth cups brown stock. Add sauce to mushrooms; cook eight minutes, and sprinkle with three tablespoons grated cheese. Arrange on circular pieces of toast.

Mushrooms à l'Italienne

Cook three tablespoons butter with one-half shallot, finely chopped, five minutes; add one-half pound mushrooms, and cook five minutes. Then add one and one-half cups canned tomatoes, drained from their liquor, and two tablespoons rolled and sifted cracker crumbs. Season with salt and pepper, and just before serving add one-third cup grated cheese and one and one-half tablespoons sherry wine. Serve on toast.

Mushrooms with Oysters

Clean twelve large, selected mushrooms; remove stems and discard; peel caps and sauté in butter. Clean one and one-half cups oysters, and cook until plump; drain, and reserve liquor. Melt two tablespoons butter, add two tablespoons flour, and pour on gradually the oyster liquor, with enough water to make one cup liquid. Add oysters, and season with one-fourth teaspoon salt and one-eighth teaspoon each celery salt and paprika. As soon as oysters are reheated pour over mushrooms.

Mushrooms and Bacon

Cut five thin slices of bacon into strips; put into a hot blazer, and cook until bacon is well browned, then remove bacon. Remove, and peel caps from eight selected mushrooms; sauté in bacon fat, and serve on circular pieces of toast. Season with salt, paprika, and a few drops onion juice; sprinkle with finely chopped parsley.

Mushrooms with Wine

Prepare one-half pound mushrooms; add three tablespoons butter and one-third cup boiling water; cover and cook slowly twelve minutes. Add one-half teaspoon salt, one eighth teaspoon paprika, a slight grating nutmeg, and one-third cup claret or hot sauterne. Serve on zephyrettes.

CHEESE DISHES

*Now good digestion wait on appetite,
And health on both*

SHAKESPEARE

XV

CHEESE DISHES

Ale Posset

MELT one tablespoon butter, add one table-spoon flour, and pour on gradually one cup milk mixed with one egg, slightly beaten. As soon as mixture thickens, add gradually one cup ale, stirring constantly. Season with salt and cayenne. This is a popular English drink on a cold winter's night, and is accompanied with toasted crackers and cheese.

English Monkey

Soak one cup stale bread crumbs in one cup milk, fifteen minutes. Melt one tablespoon butter, add one-half cup soft, mild cheese cut in small pieces, and stir until cheese has melted; then add soaked crumbs, and just before serv-ing, one egg, slightly beaten, one-half teaspoon salt, and a few grains cayenne. Pour over toasted crackers.

Chafing Dish Possibilities

Welsh Rarebit, I

Melt one tablespoon butter, add one teaspoon cornstarch, and stir until well mixed; then add one-half cup thin cream and cook two minutes. Add one-half pound soft, mild cheese, cut in small pieces, one-fourth teaspoon salt, one-half teaspoon mustard, and a few grains cayenne. Stir until cheese has melted, and mixture is of a creamy consistency. Pour over zephyrettes, or slices of bread toasted on one side, rarebit being poured over untoasted side. Rarebits may be cooked directly over the flame or over the hot water pan. An unskilled person would better select the latter.

Welsh Rarebit, II

Melt one tablespoon butter, add one-fourth teaspoon each salt and paprika, one-half teaspoon mustard and one-third cup ale or lager beer. Stir constantly, and when well heated add one-half pound mild, soft cheese cut in small pieces. Stir constantly until cheese becomes melted, and mixture is of a creamy consistency. With some cheese it is necessary to use one-half cup ale, and the additional quantity may be added during the preparation of the rarebit if the mixture seems of too thick a consistency.

Cheese Dishes

Many prefer the addition of one egg, slightly beaten, just before serving.

Golden Buck

Serve a poached egg on each portion of welsh rarebit.

Macaroni Rarebit

Follow recipe for Welsh Rarebit, I., using Young American cheese. Stir in one cup cold, cooked macaroni, broken in one-half inch pieces.

Oyster Rarebit

Clean, parboil, and drain one pint oysters, reserving the liquor. Remove and discard tough muscles. Melt two tablespoons butter, add one-half teaspoon salt, one-fourth teaspoon paprika, and pour on gradually one-half cup oyster liquor. When heated, add one-half pound soft, mild cheese cut in small pieces. Stir until mixture is smooth, then add two eggs, slightly beaten, and the oysters.

Halibut Rarebit

Rub over the inner surface of the chafing dish with a clove of garlic first dipped in salt. Melt one tablespoon butter, add one tablespoon

Chafing Dish Possibilities

cornstarch, mixed with one-half teaspoon salt
and one-fourth teaspoon paprika, then pour on
gradually one-half cup each milk and chicken
stock. Add three-fourths cup soft, mild cheese
cut in small pieces, and one cup cold, flaked,
cooked halibut. As soon as cheese is melted
add one egg slightly beaten and one and one-
half tablespoons sherry wine. Serve on slices
of toast.

Cheese Fritters

Mix four tablespoons grated Parmesan cheese
with two tablespoons stale bread crumbs. Beat
four eggs thoroughly and add to first mixture.
Season with salt and paprika. Drop from tip
of spoon in small cakes on a hot, buttered
blazer. Brown on one side, turn and brown on
the other side.

Cheese Boxes

Cut stale bread in one-third inch slices, remove
crusts, and cut slices in pieces three by one and
one-half inches. Remove centres, leaving bread
in box-shaped pieces. Fit in each box a slice
of mild cheese, sprinkle with salt and paprika,
and cover with a thin piece of bread which was
removed with the centre. Sauté in a hot blazer,
using enough butter to prevent burning.

RELISHES AND SWEETS

Who pepper'd the highest was surest to please

GOLDSMITH

Nor waste their sweetness in the desert air

CHURCHILL

XVI

RELISHES AND SWEETS

Salted Almonds

MELT one and one-half tablespoons butter and add one-fourth pound blanched Jordan almonds. Stir constantly and cook slowly until almonds are delicately browned. Drain on brown paper and sprinkle with salt. It may be necessary to remove some of the salt by wiping the nuts with an old napkin.

To Blanch Almonds

Cover almonds with boiling water and let stand two minutes; drain, put into cold water, and rub off skins. Dry between towels.

Devilled Almonds

Blanch and shred two ounces almonds. Cook until brown, using enough butter to prevent burning. Mix two tablespoons chopped pickles, one tablespoon each Chutney and Worcester-shire sauce, one-fourth teaspoon salt, and a few grains cayenne. Add to nuts, and serve as soon as thoroughly heated.

Chafing Dish Possibilities

Devilled Chestnuts

Shell one cup chestnuts and cut in thin slices. Fry until well browned, using enough butter to prevent burning. Season with Tabasco sauce.

Hamburg Cream

Mix the grated rind and juice of one-half lemon; add the yolks of four eggs, well beaten, mixed with one-half cup sugar, and cook over hot water until mixture thickens. Stir in the whites of four eggs, beaten stiff. Pour into small glasses, chill, and serve with lady fingers.

Coffee Soufflé

Mix one and one-half cups coffee infusion and one cup hot milk, in which one tablespoon granulated gelatine has been dissolved. Cook over hot water until thoroughly scalded, then add two-thirds cup sugar, one-fourth teaspoon salt, and the yolks of three eggs, slightly beaten. Stir until mixture thickens, then add the whites of three eggs beaten stiff. Turn into small moulds, previously dipped in cold water. Chill, remove from moulds, and serve with sugar and cream.

Relishes and Sweets

Macaroon Pudding

Soak twelve macaroons in sherry wine, ten minutes. Beat two eggs slightly, add four and one-half tablespoons sugar, one-fourth teaspoon salt, and one cup each milk and thin cream; then add two tablespoons blanched and chopped almonds, one-fourth teaspoon almond extract, and four finely pounded macaroons. Turn mixture into chafing dish, arrange soaked macaroons on top, cover, and cook over hot water thirty minutes.

Quick Bavarian Cream

Mix the grated rind and juice of one-half lemon, one-half cup orange juice, one-half cup sugar, and the unbeaten yolks of three eggs. Cook over hot water, stirring constantly until mixture thickens, then add the whites of two eggs, well beaten. Remove from heat, and add one-half tablespoon granulated gelatine soaked in two tablespoons cold water. Set in a pan of cold water to cool, stirring occasionally that mixture may be smooth. Line individual moulds with lady fingers, fill with mixture, and chill.

Fig Cups

Stuff one-half pound washed figs with chopped salted almonds. Put two tablespoons sugar, one teaspoon lemon juice, and one-half cup wine in blazer; when heated add figs, cover, and cook until figs are tender, turning and basting often. Serve with lady fingers.

Peach Canapés

Sauté circular pieces of sponge cake in butter until delicately browned. Drain canned peaches, sprinkle with powdered sugar, a few drops lemon juice, and a slight grating nutmeg. Melt one tablespoon butter, add peaches, and when heated serve on cake.

Bananas Cooked in the Skins

Loosen one of the sections of skin from each banana. Put into blazer, cover, and let cook until skins are discolored and pulp soft. Remove from skins and sprinkle with sugar. Serve with lady fingers.

Sautéd Bananas

Remove skins from three bananas, cut in halves lengthwise, and again cut in halves crosswise. Put one tablespoon butter in blazer; when hot add bananas and cook until soft, turning once. Drain, sprinkle with powdered sugar, and a few drops lemon juice; orange juice or sherry wine may be used if preferred.

Relishes and Sweets

Soufflé au Rhum

Beat the yolks of two eggs until thick and lemon-colored. Add three tablespoons powdered sugar and one tablespoon rum. Beat the whites of four eggs until stiff and dry, and cut and fold into the mixture. Grease blazer with clarified butter, pour in one-half the mixture and brown delicately. Fold and turn same as an omelet. Care should be taken to lift the blazer that the soufflé may brown evenly. Pour in remaining mixture and proceed as before.

Sicilian Omelet

Beat three eggs slightly, add one teaspoon sugar and a few grains salt. Grease the sides and bottom of blazer, using one-half tablespoon butter. Strain in the mixture and cook until of a creamy consistency, using a spatula to scrape cooked mixture from bottom of pan, that it may mix with the uncooked part and thus prevent any part from being overdone. Loosen omelet by running spatula around side and bottom of pan. Fold, turn, and serve with Sicilian sauce.

Sicilian Sauce

Beat one-half cup heavy cream, add one tablespoon powdered sugar, one tablespoon currant jelly, melted, and one and one-half tablespoons powdered macaroons.

Chafing Dish Possibilities

Mince Pie

Cook one and one-half cups chopped apple with one tablespoon butter, until soft. Add one-third cup each molasses and cider; then add two-thirds cup sugar mixed with one-fourth teaspoon each cinnamon, clove, and nutmeg, and one-eighth teaspoon mace. Add juice and rind of one lemon, one tablespoon vinegar, one-half cup cracker crumbs, one-third cup currants, one-third cup raisins, seeded and cut in pieces, one-fourth cup citron, cut in small strips, and salt to taste. Heat to boiling point, add three tablespoons brandy, and serve in patty shells.

Slip On

Pour welsh rarebit over mince pie.

CANDIES

The superfluous, a very necessary thing
                                                    VOLTAIRE

Sweets to the sweet ; farewell !
                                                    SHAKESPEARE

144

XVII

CANDIES

Fudge

MELT one tablespoon butter, add one-half cup milk and one and one-half cups sugar; stir until sugar is dissolved, then add five tablespoons prepared cocoa, or two squares unsweetened chocolate. Stir constantly until chocolate is melted. Heat to boiling point and boil twelve minutes, stirring occasionally to prevent burning. Extinguish flame, add one teaspoon vanilla, and beat until the mixture is creamy. Pour into a buttered pan, cool, and mark in squares.

Cocoanut Cream Candy

Melt two teaspoons butter, add one-half cup milk and one and one-half cups sugar. Heat to boiling point and boil twelve minutes, stirring occasionally to prevent burning. Extinguish flame, add one-third cup shredded cocoanut and one-half teaspoon vanilla. Beat until the mixture is creamy. Pour into a buttered pan, cool, and mark in squares.

Chafing Dish Possibilities

Lemon Taffy

Melt three-fourths tablespoon butter, and add three-fourths cup each molasses and brown sugar. Heat to boiling point, add one-eighth teaspoon cream-of-tartar, then boil twelve minutes, stirring occasionally to prevent burning. Extinguish flame, add three-fourths teaspoon lemon extract, and beat until the mixture is creamy. Pour into a buttered pan, cool, and mark in squares.

Peanut Drops

Make same as Lemon Taffy, substituting vanilla for lemon extract, and adding one-half cup peanuts, shelled and separated in halves. Drop by spoonfuls on buttered paper.

Maple Walnuts

Break three-fourths pound soft maple sugar in pieces. Put in blazer with three tablespoons boiling water and one-half cup thin cream. Heat to boiling point and boil fifteen minutes. Extinguish flame, add one-half cup English walnut meat, broken in pieces, and beat until the mixture is creamy. Pour into a buttered pan, cool, and mark in squares.

Candies

Sultana Caramels

Melt three tablespoons butter, add three table-spoons molasses, one-third cup milk, and one and one-half cups sugar. Heat to boiling point and boil eight minutes, stirring occasionally to prevent burning. Add four tablespoons pre-pared cocoa or one and one-half squares un-sweetened chocolate, and stir until chocolate is melted; then boil seven minutes. Extinguish flame, add one-third cup English walnut meat broken in pieces, one and one-half tablespoons Sultana raisins, and one-half teaspoon vanilla. Beat until the mixture is creamy, pour into a buttered pan, cool, and mark in squares.

Praulines

Heat one cup powdered sugar, one-half cup maple syrup, and one-fourth cup cream to boil-ing point, and boil until a soft ball may be formed when mixture is tried in cold water. Extinguish flame, and beat until the mixture is creamy. Add one cup pecan meat, cut in pieces, and drop from tip of spoon in small piles, on buttered paper.

Peppermints

Put one-half cup water and one and one-half cups sugar in blazer, and stir constantly until

Chafing Dish Possibilities

sugar is dissolved. Boil ten minutes. Beat until mixture begins to thicken, and add six drops oil of peppermint. Drop from tip of spoon on buttered paper, working rapidly. Should mixture become too stiff to drop, add a small quantity of boiling water.

Checkermints

Make same as Peppermints, adding oil of wintergreen instead of oil of peppermint.

Butter Taffy

Boil together one and one-half cups light brown sugar, three tablespoons molasses, one and one-half tablespoons each vinegar and hot water, and one half teaspoon salt. Cook until brittle when tried in cold water. Add three tablespoons butter, cook one minute, and add one teaspoon vanilla. Pour into a buttered pan, cool, and mark in squares.

Peanut Nougat

Put one and one-half cups sugar in blazer, and stir constantly until melted. Extinguish flame, add one cup peanut meat, chopped and sprinkled with salt. Pour into a hot buttered pan, that mixture may spread easily. Cool slightly, and mark in squares

Candies

Nut Bar

Cover the bottom of a buttered shallow pan with one and one-third cups nut meat, broken in pieces. Melt one and one-half cups sugar and pour over the nut meat. Cool slightly, and mark in bars.

French Nougat

Put one cup sugar in blazer, and stir constantly until melted, then add one-fourth pound Jordan almonds, blanched and finely chopped. Extinguish flame, add three tablespoons prepared cocoa, and stir until well mixed. Drop by spoonfuls on a buttered paper.

INDEX

INDEX

Index

Index

Index

Index

Index

Index

Index

160

Index